The Rainbow Loom® is a series of plastic pins joined together in rows. Bracelets, rings, charms & figures are made by placing elastic bands on the loom pins & looping them over each other in a pattern.

Each project has a Diagram to show where to place the bands, as well as illustrations to show looping the bands.

Below is a picture of the loom & a blank Diagram like the ones used to show band placement. Each ∪ shape represents a loom pin.

The band's color & direction are shown on the Diagram & illustrations. It's very important to follow the Steps when placing & looping the bands on the loom pins.

On the illustrations, the band that you are working with is shown in color. Bands that are in the background or not being used for that Step are shown in a much lighter color.

Several projects are made with double bands. Each time you place a band, you'll actually place **2** bands. Only **1** band is shown in the illustrations.

Joining 2 looms allows you to create wider, more complex projects, such as the Criss-Cross Bracelet. The project instructions will show you how to arrange the looms.

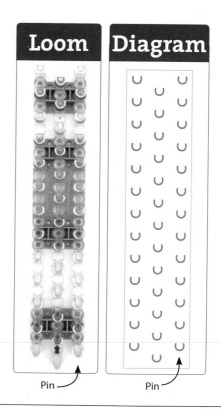

Loom **Diagram**

Pin   Pin

LEISURE ARTS, INC. • Maumelle, Arkansas

2

4

4

5

8

10

14

18

22

26

30

34

39

39

D0506585

Message Bracelet

Band Placement

When Placing the Bands:

- Place the loom on the table with the arrows pointing away from you.
- Use your fingers to place the bands on the loom & push each band down after you place it on the pins.
- Follow the Steps when placing the bands.

Step 1: Choose your letter beads & thread a band through each bead hole.

Step 2

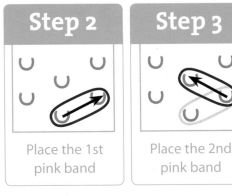

Place the 1st pink band

Step 3

Place the 2nd pink band

Step 4: Continue to place the pink & beaded bands until you reach the top of the loom (see the Diagram on page 3).

Looping

When Looping the Bands:

- Turn the loom around so the arrows are pointing toward you.
- Always use the looping tool to pick up & loop the bands.

Step 1

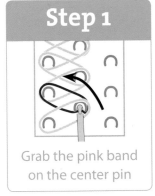

Grab the pink band on the center pin

Step 2

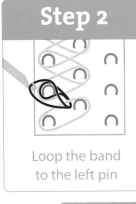

Loop the band to the left pin

Step 3

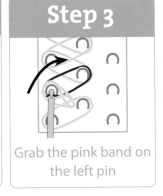

Grab the pink band on the left pin

Step 4

Loop the band to the center pin

Step 5: Continue picking up & looping the pink & beaded bands until you've looped the last pink band.

Step 6

Slide a C-clip on the pink band loops

Step 7: Carefully pull all the bands from the pins.

Step 8: Join the bracelet by slipping the C-clip through the pink loop at the beginning of the bracelet.

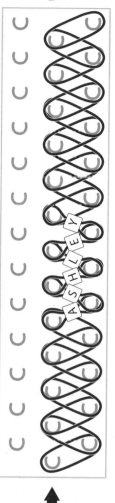

Diagram

Tip:

Share smiles with all your friends. To make a 2-color Message Bracelet, just center the beaded bands between contrasting color bands.

Earrings

The multi-hued *Circular Earrings* are easy to make on the looping tool. For each earring, follow Making Body Parts on page 48 & start with a triple twisted purple band. Then pull 1 blue band through the twisted band. Continue pulling bands through in the following order: green, yellow, orange, red, purple, blue, green, yellow, orange & red. Leave the earring on the looping tool & set aside. Open a jump ring & slide it through the loops on the tool & the twisted purple band. Slide an ear wire on the jump ring. Close the jump ring. Voila! Instant rainbow earrings!

The *Drop-style Earrings* are also made on the looping tool. For each earring, follow Making Body Parts on page 48 & start with a triple twisted pink band. Then pull a set of teal bands through the twisted band. Now just alternate pink & teal sets of bands until the earring is about 1¼" long. Open a jump ring & slide it through the top loops. Slide an ear wire on the jump ring. Close the jump ring. Make a set to match every outfit!

Loom Photo

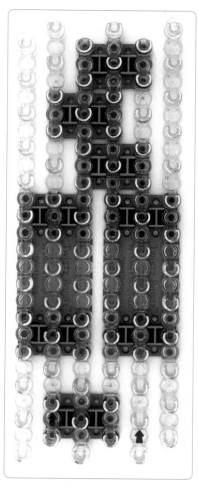

Band Placement

The illustrations show the teal, purple & pink version of this bracelet.
This open-work bracelet requires 2 looms arranged as shown in the Photo on the left.

When Placing the Bands:

- Arrange **2** looms as shown in the Photo (left).
- Place the looms on the table with the arrows pointing away from you.
- Use your fingers to place the bands on the loom & push each band down after you place it on the pins.
- Follow the Steps when placing the bands. The Diagram is on page 7.

Step 1

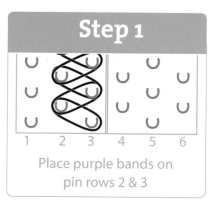

Place purple bands on
pin rows 2 & 3

Step 2

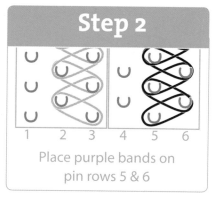

Place purple bands on
pin rows 5 & 6

Step 3

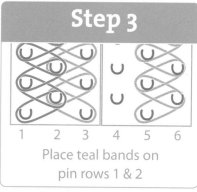

Place teal bands on
pin rows 1 & 2

Step 4

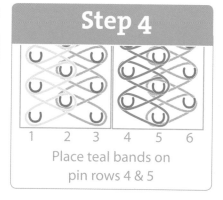

Place teal bands on
pin rows 4 & 5

Step 5

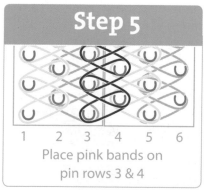

Place pink bands on
pin rows 3 & 4

Criss-Cross Ladder Bracelet continued on page 6.

Looping

When Looping the Bands:

- Turn the loom around so the arrows are pointing toward you.
- Always use the looping tool to pick up & loop the bands.

Step 1

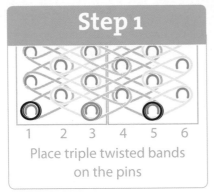

Place triple twisted bands on the pins

Step 2

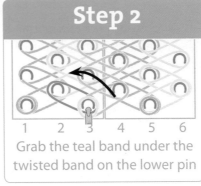

Grab the teal band under the twisted band on the lower pin

Step 3

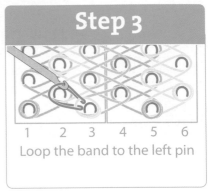

Loop the band to the left pin

Step 4

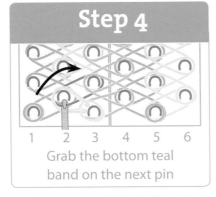

Grab the bottom teal band on the next pin

Step 5

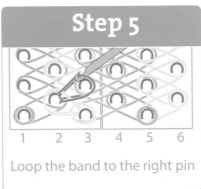

Loop the band to the right pin

Step 6: Continue picking up & looping the teal bands on pin rows 2 & 3 until you reach the top of the loom.

Step 7

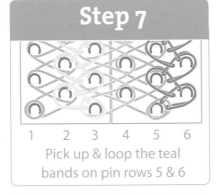

Pick up & loop the teal bands on pin rows 5 & 6

Step 8

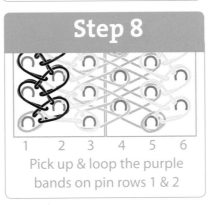

Pick up & loop the purple bands on pin rows 1 & 2

Step 9

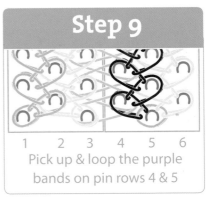

Pick up & loop the purple bands on pin rows 4 & 5

Step 10

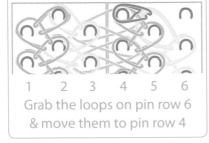

Grab the loops on pin row 6 & move them to pin row 4

Step 11: Refer to Steps 3-6 of Removing a Project from the Loom on page 46 to attach a new band to the bands on pin rows 2 & 4. Carefully remove the bracelet from the pins.

Step 12: If the bracelet is not long enough, make 2 teal Extensions (page 47).

Step 13: Join the bracelet ends with C-clips.

Diagram

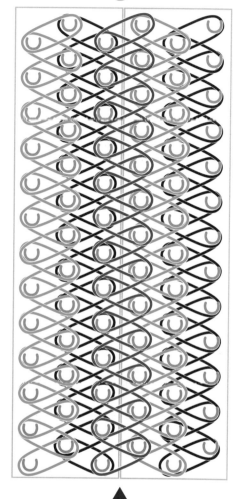

Tip:

Lime green, aqua & white are a great color combo for this bracelet. Just use the green in place of the purple, aqua in place of the teal & white instead of pink. Fun, fun, fun!

Double Triple Single Bracelet

Diagram

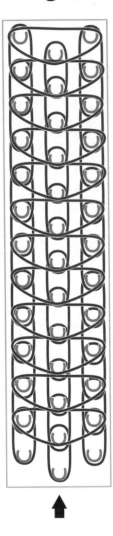

Band Placement

The illustrations show the pink version of this bracelet.
Create a lovely bracelet with a pretty gathered center.

When Placing the Bands:

- Place the loom on the table with the arrows pointing away from you.
- Each time you place a band, you'll actually place **2** bands. Only 1 band is shown in the illustrations.
- Use your fingers to place the bands on the loom & push each band down after you place it on the pins.
- Follow the Steps when placing the bands.

Steps 1-3: Place pink bands on each pin row.

Step 1	Step 2	Step 3
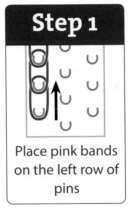	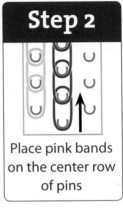	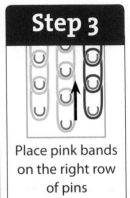
Place pink bands on the left row of pins	Place pink bands on the center row of pins	Place pink bands on the right row of pins

Step 4: Place pink bands in triangles as shown on the Diagram on the left.

Looping

When Looping the Bands:

- Turn the loom around so the arrows are pointing toward you.
- Always use the looping tool to pick up & loop the bands.

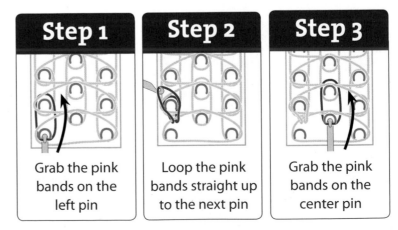

Step 1	Step 2	Step 3
Grab the pink bands on the left pin	Loop the pink bands straight up to the next pin	Grab the pink bands on the center pin

Step 4	Step 5	Step 6
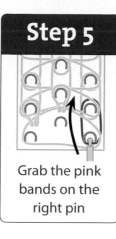	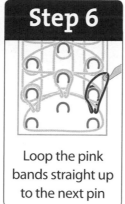	

Loop the pink bands straight up to the next pin

Grab the pink bands on the right pin

Loop the pink bands straight up to the next pin

Step 7: Continue picking up & looping the bands in the same order until you reach the top of the loom. Follow Removing a Project from the Loom on page 46 & Making A Hanging Loop on page 48 to complete the first half of the bracelet.

Step 8: Make another bracelet half, placing & looping the bands just like you did for the first half. Use one of the beginning bands to tie the two halves together at the center; clip the excess band. Slip a C-clip through the loops on the remaining ends to join the bracelet.

Mini Bag

For this mini bag, make 4 bracelets that are tied at both ends with bands (instead of a C-clip). Then, tie the bracelets together on the wrong side with more bands, placing the bands about 1/2" apart. Tie the bottom closed with bands too. Tie on a Flower Ring (page 14) & add a ribbon strap.

Turtle Charm

Band Placement

The illustrations show the green, violet & blue version of the turtle.
Hang a turtle (or a whole family of them) on your backpack.

When Placing the Bands:

- Arrange the loom as shown in the Photo (left) & place it on the table with the arrows pointing away from you.
- Each time you place a band, you'll actually place **2** bands (except for the hanging loop & for the shell stripes). Only 1 band is shown in the illustrations.
- Use your fingers to place the bands on the loom & push each band down after you place it on the pins.
- Follow the Steps when placing the bands.

Loom Photo

Step 1

For the hanging loop, place **1** green band on the pins

Step 2

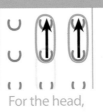

For the head, place the 1st & 2nd green bands on the pins

Step 3

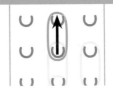

Place the 3rd green bands

Step 4

Place the 4th green bands

Step 5

For the neck, place the 5th green bands

Step 6

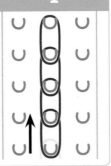

Step 6:

For the body, place 4 violet bands on the center pins

Step 7

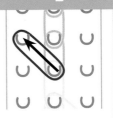

Place the 5th violet bands

Step 8

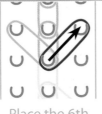

Place the 6th violet bands

Step 9

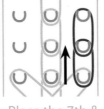

Place the 7th & 8th violet bands

Step 10

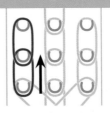

Place the 9th & 10th violet bands

Step 11

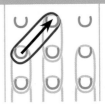

Place the 11th violet bands

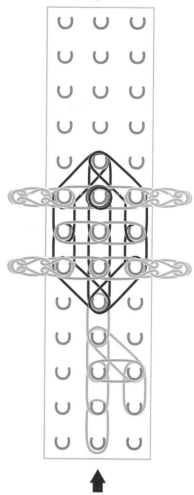

Tip:
Make a purple turtle with a blue shell & purple stripes or use tie-dye colored bands for the shell & stripes for a way cool look.

Step 12

Place the 12th violet bands

Step 13

For the eyes, place a double twisted blue band on the pins

Step 14

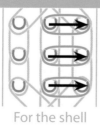

For the shell stripes, place 3 **single** blue bands

Step 15

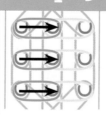

Place 3 more **single** blue bands

Step 16: For the Legs, refer to Making Body Parts on page 48 to make 4 Legs with a green triple twisted band & 2 sets of green bands on each Leg. Place the Legs on the loom as shown on the Diagram (right).

***Turtle Charm** continued on page 12.*

Looping

When Looping the Bands:

- Turn the loom around so the arrows are pointing toward you.
- Always use the looping tool to pick up & loop the bands.

Step 1

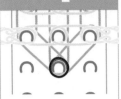

Place a triple twisted violet band on the center pin

Step 2

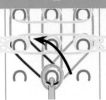

Grab the violet bands right under the twisted band

Step 3

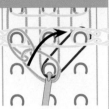

Loop the bands to the left pin

Step 4

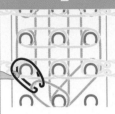

Grab the next violet bands

Step 5

Loop the bands to the right pin

Step 6

For the tail, tie a knot in the center of a green band & place it on the center pin

Step 7

Grab the violet bands on the center pin

Step 8

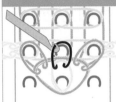

Loop the bands straight up

Step 9

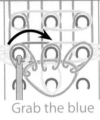

Grab the blue band on the left pin

Step 10

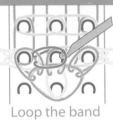

Loop the band to the center pin

Step 11

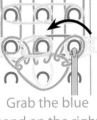

Grab the blue band on the right pin

Step 12

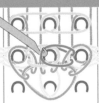

Loop the band to the center pin

Step 13

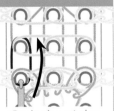

Grab the violet bands on the left pin

Step 14

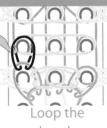

Loop the bands straight up

Step 15

Loop the next 2 violet bands straight up

Step 16

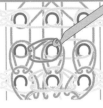

Grab the blue band on the left pin

Step 17

Loop the band to the center pin

Step 18

Grab the blue band on the right pin

Step 19

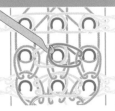

Loop the band to the center pin

Step 20:

Repeat Steps 13-19 to loop the next shell & stripes row of bands.

Step 21

Grab the violet bands on the center pin

Step 22
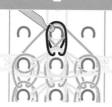
Loop the bands straight up

Step 23
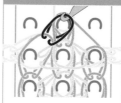
Grab the violet bands on the left pin

Step 24
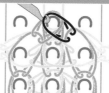
Loop the bands to the center pin

Step 25
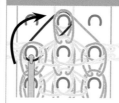
Loop the violet bands on the right pin to the center pin

Step 26
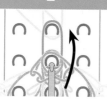
Grab the green bands on the center pin

Step 27

Loop the bands straight up

Step 28

Grab the top green bands on the center pin

Step 29
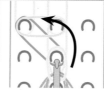
Loop the bands to the left pin

Step 30

Grab the last green bands on the center pin

Step 31

Loop the bands straight up

Step 32

Grab the bottom green bands on the next center pin

Step 33

Loop the bands straight up

Step 34
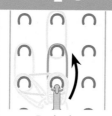
Grab the bottom green bands on the left pin

Step 35
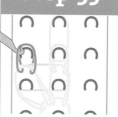
Loop the bands straight up

Step 36

Loop the bands on the left pin to the center pin

Step 37: Follow Making a Hanging Loop on page 48 to finish the Turtle. Carefully remove the Turtle from the loom.

Flower Ring

Band Placement

The illustrations show a multi-colored flower with a green base & blue beads. These beaded rings are a bit more challenging to make, so take your time & follow the Steps.

When Placing the Bands:

- Place the loom on the table with the arrows pointing away from you.
- Use your fingers to place the bands on the loom & push each band down after you place it on the pins.
- Follow the Steps when placing the bands.
- Refer to the photo on page 2 to make the beaded bands.

Step 1

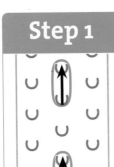

Place the 1st 2 green bands on the center pins

Step 2

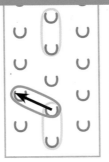

Place the 3rd green band

Step 3

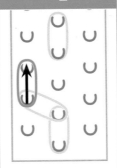

Place the 4th green band

Step 4

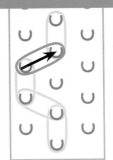

Place the 5th green band

Step 5

Place the 6th green band

Step 6

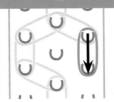

Place the 7th green band

Step 7

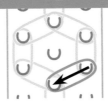

Place the 8th green band

Step 8

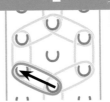

Place the 9th green band over the 3rd band to complete the base

Flower Ring continued on page 16.

Diagram

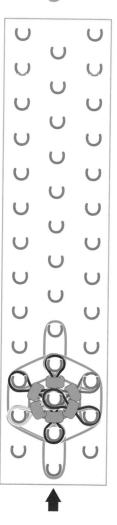

Tip:
Vary the bead or the band color (or both!) to create a whole wardrobe of rings!

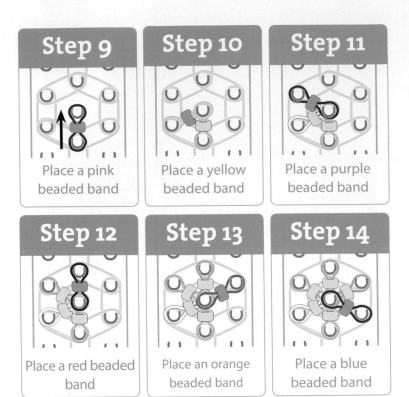

Step 9
Place a pink beaded band

Step 10
Place a yellow beaded band

Step 11
Place a purple beaded band

Step 12
Place a red beaded band

Step 13
Place an orange beaded band

Step 14
Place a blue beaded band

Looping

When Looping the Bands:

- Turn the loom around so the arrows are pointing toward you.
- Always use the looping tool to pick up & loop the bands.
- When grabbing the green bands, move the looping tool to the left a bit to grab the correct band, wiggle it out through the loops & stretch it slightly before looping to the indicated pin.

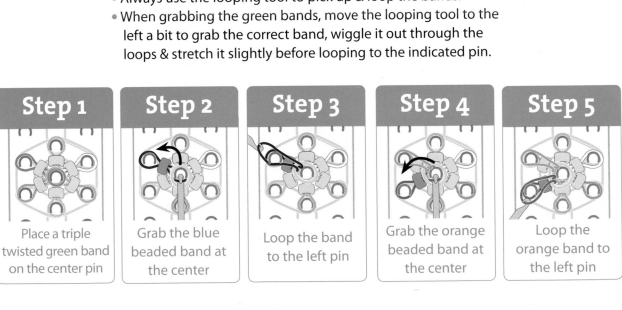

Step 1
Place a triple twisted green band on the center pin

Step 2
Grab the blue beaded band at the center

Step 3
Loop the band to the left pin

Step 4
Grab the orange beaded band at the center

Step 5
Loop the orange band to the left pin

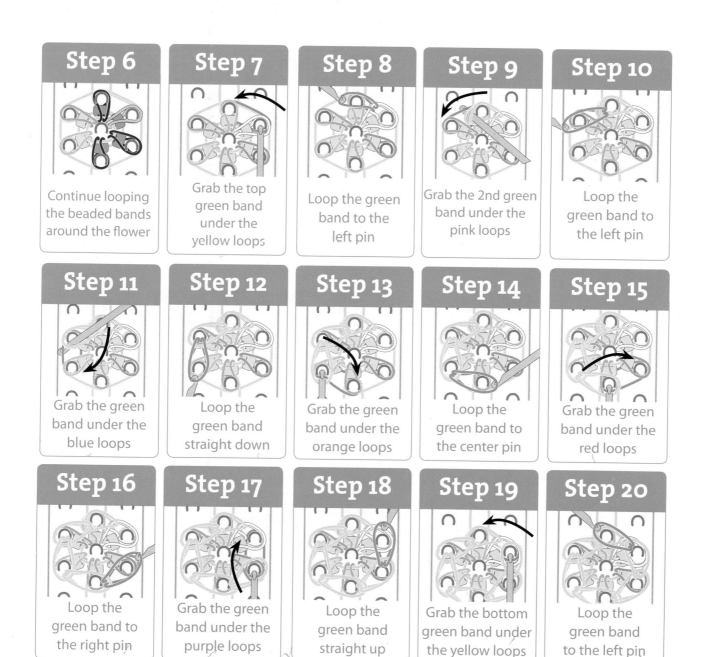

Step 6
Continue looping the beaded bands around the flower

Step 7
Grab the top green band under the yellow loops

Step 8
Loop the green band to the left pin

Step 9
Grab the 2nd green band under the pink loops

Step 10
Loop the green band to the left pin

Step 11
Grab the green band under the blue loops

Step 12
Loop the green band straight down

Step 13
Grab the green band under the orange loops

Step 14
Loop the green band to the center pin

Step 15
Grab the green band under the red loops

Step 16
Loop the green band to the right pin

Step 17
Grab the green band under the purple loops

Step 18
Loop the green band straight up

Step 19
Grab the bottom green band under the yellow loops

Step 20
Loop the green band to the left pin

Step 21: Follow Making A Hanging Loop on page 48 to secure the top & bottom bands. Carefully remove the ring from the loom. Slip the loops over your finger to wear the ring.

6-Row Fishtail Cuff

Loom Photo

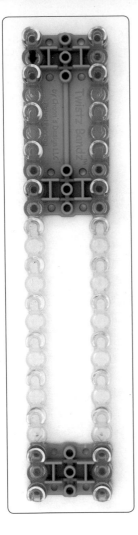

Band Placement

The illustrations show the black, blue, pink & orange version of the bracelet.
A simple locking band placed every 3 rows stabilzes this wide cuff.

When Placing the Bands:

- Remove the center row of pins & arrange the loom as shown in the Photo (left).
- Place the loom on the table with the arrows pointing **toward** you.
- Use your fingers to place the bands on the loom & push each band down after you place it on the pins.
- Follow the Steps when placing the bands.

Step 1	Step 2	Step 3	Step 4
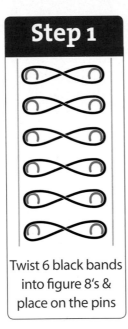	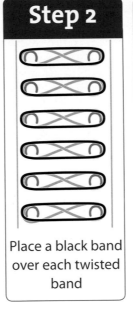	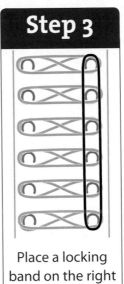	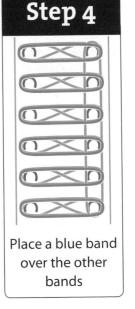
Twist 6 black bands into figure 8's & place on the pins	Place a black band over each twisted band	Place a locking band on the right pins	Place a blue band over the other bands

6-Row Fishtail Cuff continued on page 20.

Diagram

Tip:

It's easy to change this bracelet to 2 colors. Just place violet bands instead of the blue, orange & pink bands.

Looping

When Looping the Bands:
- Always use the looping tool to pick up & loop the bands.
- Push the bands down on the pins after you loop them.

Step 1
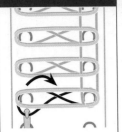
Grab the bottom black band on the lower left pin

Step 2
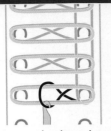
Loop the band to the center over the other bands

Step 3

Loop the remaining 5 bands to the center

Step 4
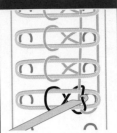
Go behind the locking band & grab the bottom black band on the lower right pin

Step 5
Loop the band to the center over the other bands

Step 6
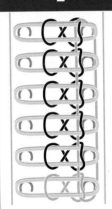
Loop the remaining 5 bands to the center

Step 7
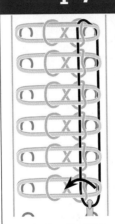
Grab the locking band on the lower right pin

Step 8
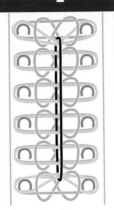
Loop the locking band to the center over the other bands

Step 9
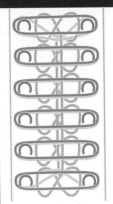
Place 6 blue bands on the pins

Step 10
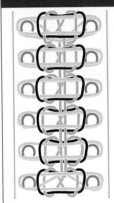
Loop the bottom black bands to the center

Step 11
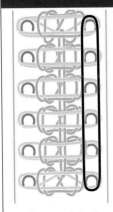
Place a black locking band on the pins

Step 12
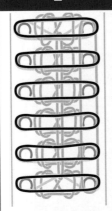
Place 6 black bands on the pins

Step 13
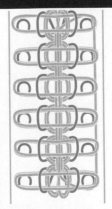
Loop bottom blue bands to the center

Step 14

Grab the locking band on the lower right pin

Step 15
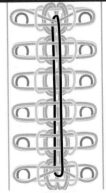
Loop the locking band to the center over the other bands

Step 16

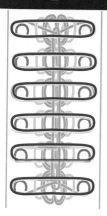

Place 6 pink bands on the pins

Step 17:

Continue looping & placing bands & locking bands referring to the photo on page 19 for color sequence. When the bracelet is long enough, loop the bottom bands to the center, leaving 1 band on each pin.

Step 18

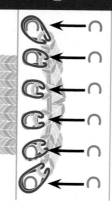

Loop the bands on the right pins to the left pins

Step 19

start here

Place 6 black bands on the right pins

Step 20

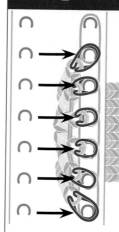

Loop the bands on the left pins back to the right pins

Step 21

Bring the bracelet around the loom & place the beginning bands on the right pins

Step 22

To join the bracelet, grab the bottom black band on the right pin

Step 23

Loop the band straight up

Step 24

Loop the next 4 black bands straight up

Step 25:

Follow Making a Hanging Loop on page 48 to secure the last black band.

Step 26:

Remove the pin row from the blue bases & carefully pull the bracelet from the pins.

Step 27

Bring the hanging loop to the wrong side of the bracelet. Slide a C-clip on it & one of the bands at the opposite end.

Chevron Bracelet

Loom Photo

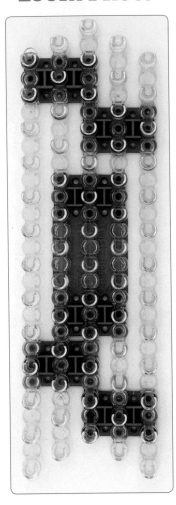

Band Placement

The illustrations show the navy, orange, pink & green version of the bracelet (shown at the top right on page 23).

Using a dark color like navy or black defines the bracelet edges & lets the brightly colored chevrons stand out.

When Placing the Bands:

- Arrange **2** looms as shown in the Photo (left).
- Place the loom on the table with the arrows pointing away from you.
- Use your fingers to place the bands on the loom & push each band down after you place it on the pins.
- Follow the Steps when placing the bands.

Step 1

Place navy bands on the far left pins

Step 2

Place navy bands on the far right pins

Step 3

Place the 1st diagonal navy band on the pins

Step 4

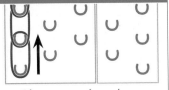

Place the 2nd diagonal navy band on the pins

Step 5

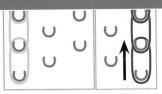

Place the 3rd diagonal navy band on the pins

Step 6

Place the 4th diagonal navy band on the pins

Step 7: Repeat Steps 3-6 to place diagonal navy bands to the top of the loom.

Step 8

For the color stripe, place the 1st orange band on the pins

Step 9

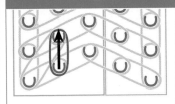

Place the 2nd orange band on the pins

Step 10

Place the 3rd orange band on the pins

Chevron Bracelet continued on page 24.

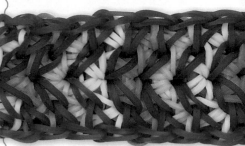

Diagram

Tip:
To make a rainbow colored chevron bracelet, place a different rainbow color on each row instead of alternating 3 colors.

Step 11

Step 12

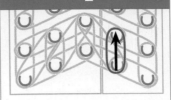
Step 13

Step 14

Place the 4th orange band on the pins

Place the 5th orange band on the pins

Place the 6th orange band on the pins

Place the 7th orange band on the pins

Step 15: Continue to place the stripe bands to the top of the loom, referring to the Diagram & photo at the top of page 23 for the color sequence.

Looping
When Looping the Bands:
- Turn the loom around so the arrows are pointing toward you.
- Always use the looping tool to pick up & loop the bands.
- When grabbing each band, wiggle the band out through the loops & stretch it slightly before looping to the indicated pin.

Step 1

Place triple twisted navy bands on the pins & triple twisted matching color bands on the center pins

Step 2

Grab the top green band on the left pin

Step 3
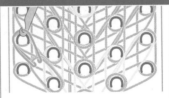

Loop the band to the far left pin

Step 4

Grab the remaining green band on the left pin

Step 5

Loop the band straight up

Step 6

Grab the top green band on the center pin

Step 7

Loop the band to the left pin

Step 8

Grab the next green band on the center pin

Step 9

Loop the band straight up

Step 10

Grab the last green band on the center pin

Step 11

Loop the band to the right pin

Step 12

Grab the top green band on the right pin

Step 13

Loop the band straight up

Step 14

Grab the last green band on the right pin

Step 15

Loop the band to the far right pin

Step 16: Continue picking up & looping the color stripe bands to the top of the loom.

Step 17

Go back to the loom bottom & grab the top navy band under the twisted band on the center pin

Step 18

Loop the band to the left pin

Step 19

Grab the bottom navy band on the left pin

Step 20

Loop the band to the far left pin

Step 21

Grab the navy band on the center pin

Step 22

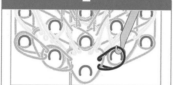

Loop the band to the right pin

Step 23

Grab the bottom navy band on the right pin

Step 24

Loop the band to the far right pin

Step 25: Continue picking up & looping the diagonal navy bands to the top of the loom.

Step 26

Go back to the loom bottom & loop the navy bands on the far left pin row straight up to the top of the loom

Step 27

Go back to the loom bottom & loop the navy bands on the far right pin row straight up to the top of the loom

Step 28: Follow Steps 3-7 of Removing a Project from the Loom on page 46 to pull a new band through the bands on the far left pin & far right pin. Follow Making a Bracelet Extension on page 47 to complete the bracelet.

Owl Charm

Band Placement

The illustrations show the brown & orange version of the owl. Whooo's your favorite friend to hang out with? These owl charms make great gifts for your friends.

When Placing the Bands:

- Place the loom on the table with the arrows pointing away from you.
- Use your fingers to place the bands on the loom & push each band down after you place it on the pins.
- Follow the Steps when placing the bands.

Step 1	Step 2	Step 3	Step 4
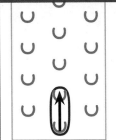	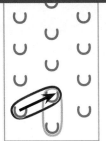		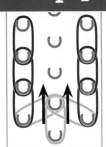
Place the 1st brown band on the center pins	Place the 2nd brown band on the pins	Place the 3rd brown band on the pins	Place the 4th-9th brown bands on the pins

Step 5	Step 6	Step 7	Step 8	Step 9
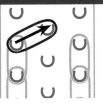			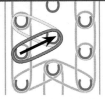	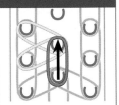
Place the 10th brown band on the pins	Place the 11th brown band on the pins	Place the 1st orange band on the pins	Place the 2nd orange band on the pins	Place the 3rd orange band on the pins

Step 10	Step 11	Step 12	Step 13	Step 14
	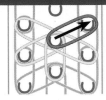	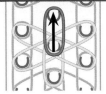	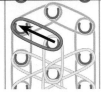	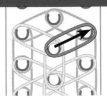
Place the 4th orange band on the pins	Place the 5th orange band on the pins	Place the 6th orange band on the pins	Place the 7th orange band on the pins	Place the 8th orange band on the pins

Diagram

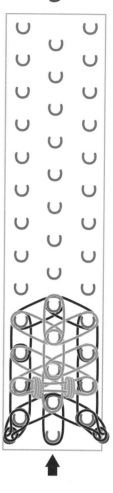

Step 15

Place the 9th orange band on the pins

Step 16:
For the Eyes, refer to Steps 1-4 of Making Body Parts on page 48 to place 2 triple twisted green bands on a brown band. Place the band as shown on the Diagram (right). For each Ear Tuft, place a triple twisted brown band on a brown band. Place the Tufts on the pins as shown.

Tip:
An owl with dark orange & light orange bands is a great companion to the brown & orange owl.

Owl Charm continued on page 28.

Looping

When Looping the Bands:

- Turn the loom around so the arrows are pointing toward you.
- Always use the looping tool to pick up & loop the bands.

Step 1
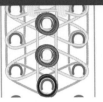
Place triple twisted brown & orange bands on the pins

Step 2
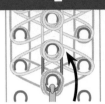
Grab the orange band on the center pin

Step 3

Loop the band straight up

Step 4

Grab the 3rd to bottom orange band on the next center pin

Step 5

Loop the band to the left pin

Step 6

Grab the 2nd to bottom orange band on the center pin

Step 7

Loop the band to the right pin

Step 8

Grab the bottom orange band on the center pin

Step 9
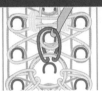
Loop the band straight up

Step 10

Grab the 1st orange band under the twisted band on the next center pin

Step 11

Loop the band to the left pin

Step 12
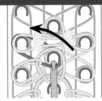
Grab the next orange band on the center pin

Step 13

Loop the band to the left pin

Step 14
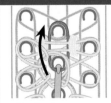
Grab the next orange band on the center pin

Step 15

Loop the band straight up

Step 16
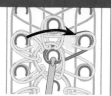
Grab the next orange band on the center pin

Step 17

Loop the band to the right pin

Step 18

Grab the last orange band on the center pin

Step 19

Loop the band to the right pin

Step 20
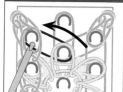
Grab the 1st brown band under the twisted band on the center pin

Step 21

Loop the band to the left pin

Step 22
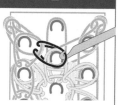
Grab the bottom brown band on the left pin

Step 23

Loop the band straight up

Step 24:
Pick up & loop the remaining 2 brown bands on the left side.

Step 25
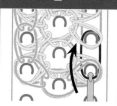
Grab the bottom brown band on the left pin

Step 26
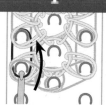
Loop the band to the center pin

Step 27

Go back to the loom bottom & grab the bottom brown band on the center pin

Step 28

Loop the band to the right pin

Step 29

Grab the bottom brown band on the right pin

Step 30
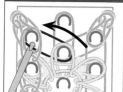
Loop the band straight up

Step 31:
Pick up & loop the remaining 2 brown bands on the right side.

Step 32
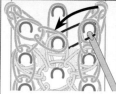
Grab the bottom brown band on the right pin

Step 33
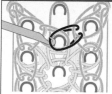
Loop the band to the center pin

Step 34:
Follow Making a Hanging Loop on page 48 to finish the Owl. Carefully remove the Owl from the loom.

Whale Charm

Band Placement

The illustrations show the black, teal & white whale. The shark has a few differences. See the Diagram & information on page 31 to make the Shark. You'll have a whale of a good time making these charms for your keys.

When Placing the Bands:

- Place the loom on the table with the arrows pointing away from you.
- Each time you place a band, you'll actually place **2** bands. Only 1 band is shown in the illustrations.
- Use your fingers to place the bands on the loom & push each band down after you place it on the pins.
- Follow the Steps when placing the bands.

Step 1

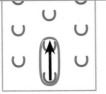

Place teal bands on the center pins

Step 2

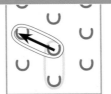

For the lower body, place the 1st white bands on the pins

Step 3

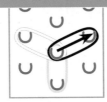

For the upper body, place the 1st black bands on the pins

Step 4

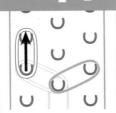

Place lower body white bands on the left pins

Step 5:
Place 7 more sets of white bands on the left pins as shown on the Diagram (right).

Step 6

Place mid body teal bands on the center pins

Step 7:
Place 8 more sets of teal bands on the center pins as shown on the Diagram.

Step 8

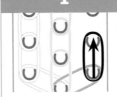

Place upper body black bands on the right pins

Step 9:
Place 7 more sets of black bands on the right pins as shown on the Diagram.

Step 10

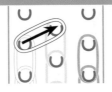

Place **1** white band on the pins

Step 11

Place **1** black band on the pins

Step 12

For the lower tail, place white bands on the pins

Whale Charm continued on page 32.

Whale Diagram

Shark Diagram

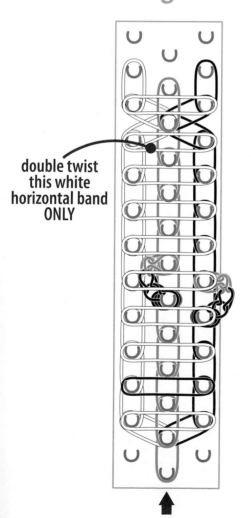

double twist this white horizontal band ONLY

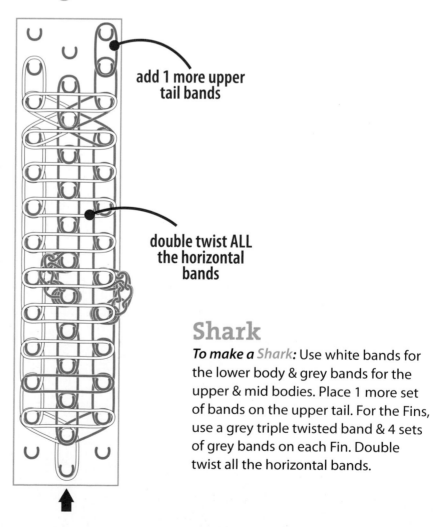

add 1 more upper tail bands

double twist ALL the horizontal bands

Shark

To make a Shark: Use white bands for the lower body & grey bands for the upper & mid bodies. Place 1 more set of bands on the upper tail. For the Fins, use a grey triple twisted band & 4 sets of grey bands on each Fin. Double twist all the horizontal bands.

Step 13

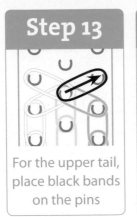

For the upper tail, place black bands on the pins

Step 14

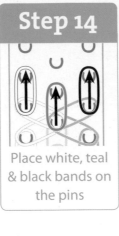

Place white, teal & black bands on the pins

Step 15: For the Fins, refer to Making Body Parts on page 48 to make 2 Fins with a black triple twisted band, 2 sets of black bands & 2 sets of teal bands on each Fin. Place the Fins on the loom.

Step 16

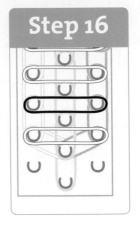

Step 16: Place white & black bands on the loom as shown on the Diagram on page 31.

Looping

When Looping the Bands:

- Turn the loom around so the arrows are pointing toward you.
- Always use the looping tool to pick up & loop the bands.

Step 1

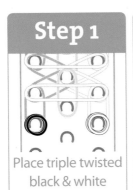

Place triple twisted black & white bands on the pins

Step 2

Grab the bottom black bands on the left pin

Step 3

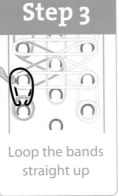

Loop the bands straight up

Step 4

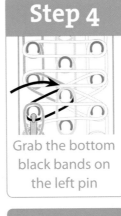

Grab the bottom black bands on the left pin

Step 5

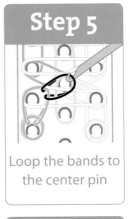

Loop the bands to the center pin

Step 6

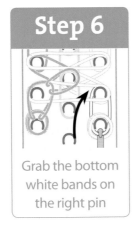

Grab the bottom white bands on the right pin

Step 7

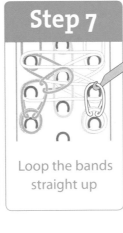

Loop the bands straight up

Step 8

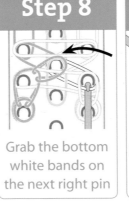

Grab the bottom white bands on the next right pin

Step 9

Loop the bands to the center pin

Step 10

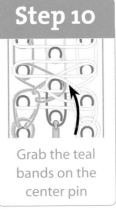

Grab the teal bands on the center pin

Step 11

Loop the bands straight up

Step 12

Grab the bottom black band on the center pin

Step 13
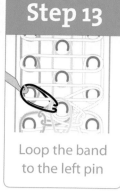
Loop the band to the left pin

Step 14
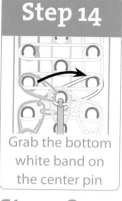
Grab the bottom white band on the center pin

Step 15

Loop the band to the right pin

Step 16
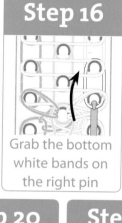
Grab the bottom white bands on the right pin

Step 17
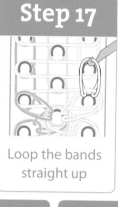

Loop the bands straight up

Step 18:
Loop the remaining 7 white band sets on the right pins.

Step 19
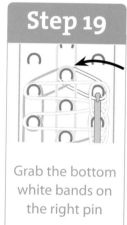
Grab the bottom white bands on the right pin

Step 20

Loop the bands to the center pin

Step 21

Go back to the loom bottom & grab the bottom teal bands on the center pin

Step 22

Loop the bands straight up

Step 23:
Loop the remaining 8 teal band sets on the center pins.

Step 24

Go back to the loom bottom & grab the bottom black bands on the left pin

Step 25
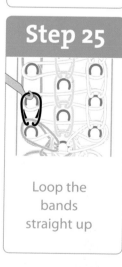
Loop the bands straight up

Step 26:
Loop the remaining 7 black band sets on the left pins.

Step 27
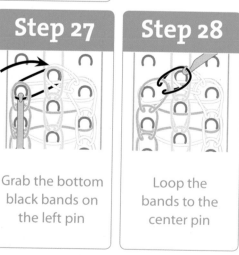
Grab the bottom black bands on the left pin

Step 28
Loop the bands to the center pin

Step 29:
Follow Making a Hanging Loop on page 48 to finish the Whale. Carefully remove the Whale from the loom.

33

Double Starburst Bracelet

Loom Photo

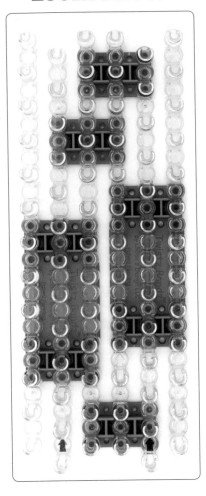

Band Placement

The illustrations show the light blue, dark blue, pink & green version of the bracelet. Double Starbursts are created on 2 looms.

When Placing the Bands:

- Arrange **2** looms as shown in the Photo (left).
- Place the loom on the table with the arrows pointing away from you.
- Use your fingers to place the bands on the loom & push each band down after you place it on the pins.
- Follow the Steps when placing the bands.

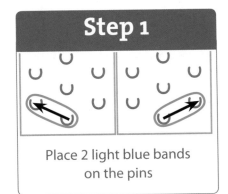

Step 1

Place 2 light blue bands on the pins

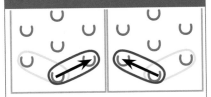

Step 2

Place 2 dark blue bands on the pins

Step 3

Beginning with dark blue & alternating dark blue & light blue, place 11 bands on each outer pin row

Step 4: Refer to the Diagram on page 35 to place light blue & dark blue diagonal bands on the pins at the top of the loom.

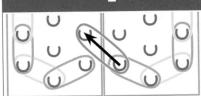

Step 5

For the center row, place a light blue band on the pins

Double Starburst Bracelet continued on page 36.

Diagram

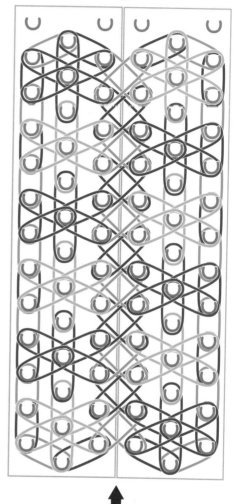

Tip:

With all the new types (jelly, tie-dye, glow-in-the-dark) of bands available, you can design all sorts of bracelets bursting with color! Try mixing violet, teal, black & clear for a semi-transparent look.

Step 6

Place the 2nd
light blue band
on the pins

Step 7

Beginning with dark
blue & alternating dark
blue & light blue, place
10 more sets of bands

Step 8

For the left starburst,
place the 1st green
band on the pins

Step 9

Place the 2nd green
band on the pins

Step 10

Place the 3rd green
band on the pins

Step 11

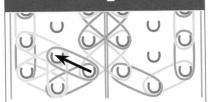

Place the 4th green
band on the pins

Step 12

Place the 5th green
band on the pins

Step 13

Place the 6th green
band on the pins

Step 14

Repeat Steps 8-13 to
place 6 pink bands

Step 15:

Continue to place
green & pink bands on
the pins until you reach
the top of the loom
(see the Diagram on
page 35).

Step 16

Beginning with pink, place the
starburst bands on the right
side of the loom

Looping
When Looping the Bands:
- Turn the loom around so the arrows are pointing toward you.
- Always use the looping tool to pick up & loop the bands.

Step 1

Place triple twisted dark blue bands on the lower pins & a triple twisted contrasting color band on each starburst center pin

Step 2
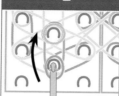
Grab the green band on the lower center pin on the left side

Step 3

Loop the band straight up

Step 4
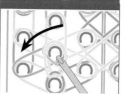
Grab the 2nd green band under the twisted band on the starburst center pin

Step 5

Loop the band to the left pin

Step 6
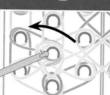
Grab the next green band on the starburst center pin

Step 7

Loop the band to the left pin

Step 8

Grab the next green band on the starburst center pin

Step 9

Loop the band straight up

Step 10

Grab the next green band on the starburst center pin

Step 11

Loop the band to the right pin

Step 12

Grab the last green band on the starburst center pin

Step 13

Loop the band to the right pin

Step 14:
Repeat Steps 2-13 to loop the pink & green starburst bands on the left side pins until you reach the top of the loom.

Step 15:
Go back to the loom bottom & repeat Steps 2-13 to loop the pink & green starburst bands on the right side pins until you reach the top of the loom.

Step 16

Go back to the loom bottom & grab the light blue band on the right pin

Step 17

Loop the band to the left pin

Step 18
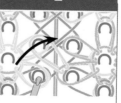
Grab the light blue band on the left pin

Double Starburst Bracelet continued on page 38.

Step 19

Loop the band to the right pin

Step 20

Loop the light blue & dark blue bands to the top of the loom

Step 21

Go back down to the loom bottom & grab the dark blue band on the left

Step 22

Loop the band to the left center pin

Step 23

Grab the light blue band on the left center pin

Step 24

Loop the band to the far left pin

Step 25

Grab the dark blue band on the far left pin

Step 26

Loop the band straight up

Step 27

Loop the light blue & dark blue bands to the top of the loom

Step 28

At the top of the loom, loop the light blue band on the far left pin to the left center pin

Step 29
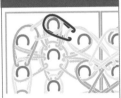
Loop the dark blue band on the right pin to the center pin

Step 30

Go back down to the loom bottom & grab the dark blue band on the left pin

Step 31

Loop the band to the right center pin

Step 32

Grab the light blue band on the right center pin

Step 33

Loop the band to the far right pin

Step 34

Grab the dark blue band on the far right pin

Step 35

Loop the band straight up

Step 36

Loop the light blue & dark blue bands to the top of the loom

Step 37

At the top of the loom, loop the light blue band on the far right pin to the right center pin

Step 38

Loop the dark blue band on the left pin to the right center pin

Step 39: Refer to Steps 3-7 of Removing a Project from the Loom on page 46, placing the loops from the 2 center pins on the looping tool. Follow Making a Bracelet Extension on page 47 to make 2 extensions, completing the bracelet.

Figures

The basic band placement & looping is similar for any of these fun figures. We show how to make a Boy, but it is easy to create a Girl, Bear, or Panda. Simply add pigtails for a Girl & change out some of the band colors for her clothes. For a Bear or Panda, refer to the Diagram for colors & to add ears. You can also make your favorite Super Hero just by changing the band colors. Because the figures are made with double bands, they are sturdy, yet flexible.

Boy Diagram

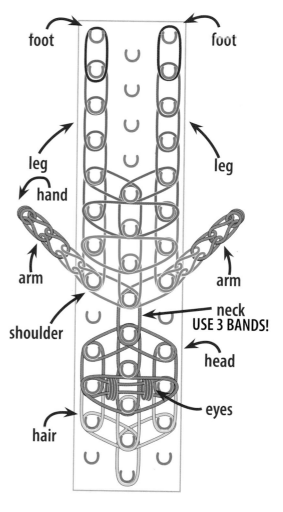

foot · foot · leg · hand · leg · arm · arm · shoulder · neck USE 3 BANDS! · head · eyes · hair

Figures continued on page 40.

Girl Diagram

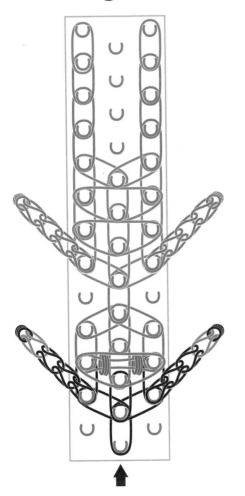

Panda Diagram

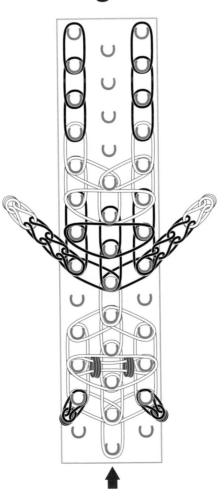

Bear Diagram

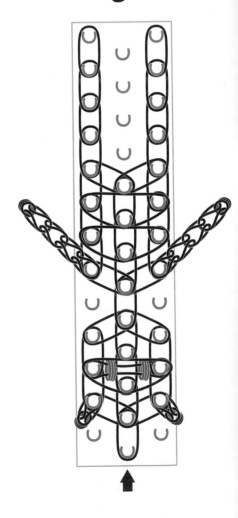

Boy

Band Placement
When Placing the Bands:

- Place the loom on the table with the arrows pointing away from you.
- Each time you place a band, you'll actually place **2** bands. Only 1 band is shown in the illustrations.
- Use your fingers to place the bands on the loom & push each band down after you place it on the pins.
- Follow the Steps when placing the bands.
- Diagram is on page 39.

Step 1

For the hair, place the 1st yellow bands

Step 2
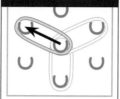
Place the 2nd yellow bands

Step 3
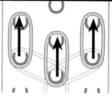
Place the 3rd yellow bands

Step 4

Place the 4th, 5th & 6th yellow bands

Step 5
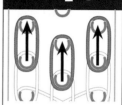
For the head, place the 1st, 2nd & 3rd light orange bands

Step 6

Place the 4th light orange bands

Step 7
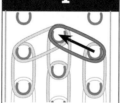
Place the 5th light orange bands

Step 8
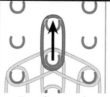
Place the 6th light orange bands

Step 9
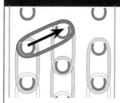
For the neck, place **3** light orange bands on the center pins

Step 10

For the shoulders, place the 1st green bands (shirt/chest)

Step 11
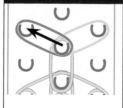
Place the 2nd green bands

Step 12
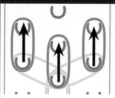
Place the 3rd, 4th & 5th green bands

Step 13
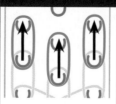
Place the 6th, 7th & 8th green bands

Step 14

For the pants, place the 1st, 2nd & 3rd navy bands (lower body color)

Step 15

Place the 4th navy bands

Boy continued on page 42.

Step 16

Place the 5th navy bands

Step 17

For the pant legs, place the 1st & 2nd navy bands

Step 18
Place the 3rd & 4th navy bands

Step 19
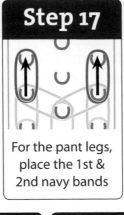
Place the 5th & 6th navy bands

Step 20
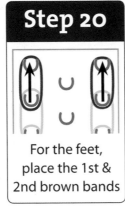
For the feet, place the 1st & 2nd brown bands

Step 21
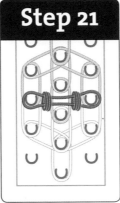

Step 21: For the Eyes, refer to Steps 1-4 of Making Body Parts on page 48 to place 2 triple twisted eye color bands on a head color band. Place the band as shown.

Step 22

Step 23
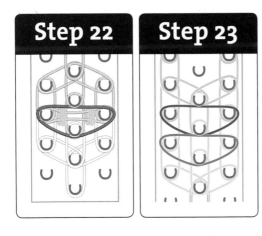

Step 22-23: Place double twisted matching color bands on the loom in triangles as shown.

Step 24: For the Arms, refer to Making Body Parts on page 48 to make 2 Arms with a light orange twisted band for the hand, 2 sets of light orange bands for the lower arms & 2 sets of green bands for the sleeves on each Arm.

Step 25: Place the Arms on the loom as shown on the Diagram (page 39).

To make a Girl Figure: Use a light orange twisted band for the hand & 4 sets of light orange bands to make each Arm. Make 2 brown Pigtails with a brown twisted band, 1 set of aqua bands & 3 sets of brown bands for each Pigtail. Place the Arms & Pigtails on the loom as shown on the Diagram (page 40).

To make a Bear or Panda Figure: Referring to the photo & Diagram (page 40) for colors, use a triple twisted band for the paw & 4 sets of bands to make each Arm. Use a triple twisted band & 1 set of bands to make each Ear. Place the Arms & Ears on the loom as shown on the Diagram.

Looping

When Looping the Bands:

- Turn the loom around so the arrows are pointing toward you.
- Always use the looping tool to pick up & loop the bands.

Step 1

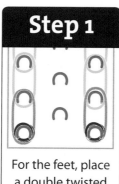

For the feet, place a double twisted brown band on the left & right pins

Step 2

Grab the bottom brown bands on the left pin

Step 3

Loop the bands straight up

Step 4

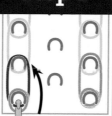

Loop the navy pant leg bands straight up

Step 5

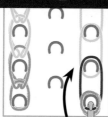

Grab the bottom brown bands on the right pin

Step 6

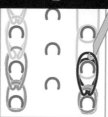

Loop the bands straight up

Step 7

Loop the navy pant leg bands straight up

Step 8

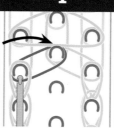

Grab the navy lower body bands on the left pin

Boy continued on page 44.

Step 9

Loop the bands to the center pin

Step 10

Grab the navy lower body bands on the right side

Step 11

Loop the bands to the center pin

Step 12
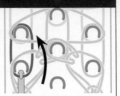
Grab the next navy bands on the left pin

Step 13

Loop the bands straight up

Step 14

Grab the next 2 green shirt bands & loop them straight up

Step 15

Grab the navy bands on the center pin

Step 16

Loop the bands straight up

Step 17

Grab the next 2 green shirt bands & loop them straight up

Step 18
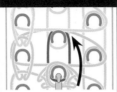
Grab the navy bands on the right pin

Step 19

Loop the bands straight up

Step 20
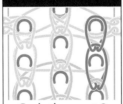
Grab the next 2 green shirt bands & loop them straight up

Step 21

Grab the green shoulder bands on the right pin

Step 22

Loop the bands to the center pin

Step 23

Grab the green shoulder bands on the left pin

Step 24

Loop the bands to the center pin

Step 25

Grab the light orange neck bands on the center pin

Step 26

Loop the bands straight up

Step 27

Grab the top light orange head bands on the center pin

Step 28

Loop the bands to the left pin

Step 29
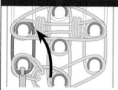
Grab the light orange head bands on the left pin

Step 30

Loop the bands straight up

Step 31
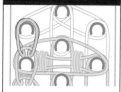
Loop the yellow hair bands on the left pin straight up

Step 32
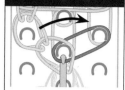
Grab the light orange head bands on the center pin

Step 33

Loop the bands to the right pin

Step 34

Grab the light orange head bands on the left pin

Step 35

Loop the bands straight up

Step 36

Loop the yellow hair bands on the right pin straight up

Step 37

Grab the light orange head bands on the center pin

Step 38

Loop the bands straight up

Step 39

Loop the yellow hair bands on the center pin straight up

Step 40

Grab the yellow hair bands on the left pin

Step 41

Loop the bands to the center pin

Step 42

Grab the yellow hair bands on the right pin

Step 43

Loop the bands to the center pin

Step 44: Follow Making a Hanging Loop on page 48 to finish the Boy. Carefully remove the Boy from the loom.

Removing a Project from the Loom

Sometimes you'll need to remove a project that still has unlooped bands from the loom. Here's how to loop & remove the project.

Step 1
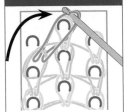
Grab & move the left loops to the center pin

Step 2
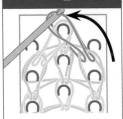
Grab & move the right loops to the center pin

Step 3
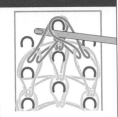
Grab all the loops on the center pin

Step 4
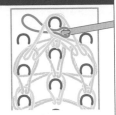
Pull a new band halfway through the loops

Step 5
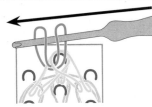
Slide the looping tool through the opposite end of the new band

Step 6
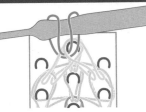
Position the loops on the indented section of the looping tool

Step 7:
Carefully remove the project from the pins & set aside.

Making a Bracelet Extension

Band Placement

Some bracelets need an extension to be long enough to wear; the project instructions will tell when to make one. The extension is made on the loom pins.

When Placing the Bands:

- Turn the loom so the open side of the pins is facing away from you.
- Starting at the loom bottom, use your fingers to place the bands on the loom (refer to your project instructions for band color & see the Diagram on the right).
- Push each band down after you place it on the pins.

Looping

When Looping the Bands:

- Turn the loom around so the open side of the pins is facing you.
- Always use the looping tool to pick up & loop the bands.

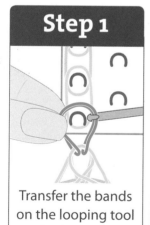

Step 1

Transfer the bands on the looping tool to the bottom pin

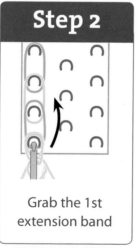

Step 2

Grab the 1st extension band

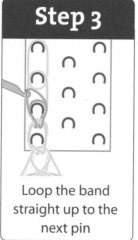

Step 3

Loop the band straight up to the next pin

Step 4: Continue picking up & looping the extension bands until you loop the last band.

Step 5

Slide a C-clip on the band loops

Step 6: Pull the band with the C-clip off the pin. Carefully pull all the bands from the pins. Join the bracelet by slipping the C-clip through the loop (or loops) at the other end of the bracelet.

Diagram

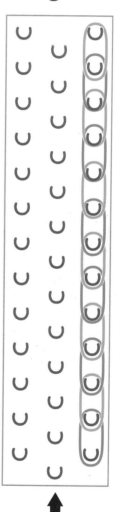

Making Body Parts

Step 1

Place a band on the looping tool & twist

Step 2a

Bring the twist up to the hook

Step 2b

Place the twist on the hook (2 twists on hook)

Step 3a

Twist the band again

Step 3b

Place the twist on the hook (3 twists on the hook)

Step 4a

Place a new band (or 2) on the hook

Step 4b
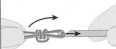
Pull the band(s) halfway through the triple twisted band

Step 4c

Place both loops on the hook

Step 5

Place a new band (or 2) on the hook & pull halfway through

Step 6

Place both loops on the hook

Step 7: Continue adding new bands until the body part is long enough (the project instructions will tell you). Place the body part as indicated in the project instructions & on the Diagram.

Making a Hanging Loop

Step 1

Grab the bottom band(s)

Step 2
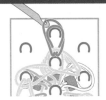
Loop the band(s) straight up to the center pin

Step 3

Grab the bottom band(s) & pull it through the top band(s)

Step 4
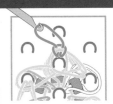
Remove the bands from the pin & pull the loop to tighten

Production Team: Designer – Kelly Reider; Technical Writer – Mary Sullivan Hutcheson; Technical Associate – Jean Lewis; Editorial Writer – Susan Frantz Wiles; Senior Graphic Artist – Lora Puls; Lead Graphic Artist – Jessica Bramlett; Graphic Artist – Cailen Cochran; Photostylist – Lori Wenger; Photographers – Jason Masters and Ken West.